Binna Burra Bell

Also by Catherine McLeod:

Wednesday is Jim Day
(2019, Whortleberry Books and Manuscripts, Garvoc, VIC
ISBN 9780648562702)

Lucila Zentner's artwork can be seen at:

Website: lucilazentnerart.com
Instagram: @lucilazentner

Binna Burra Bell

Written by Catherine McLeod
Illustrated by Lucila Zentner
Edited by Eleanor Whitworth

PenFolk Publishing, Blackburn Victoria
October 2025

Published for Catherine McLeod and Binna Burra Foundation in October 2025 by
PenFolk Publishing
21 Ronley Street
Blackburn Victoria 3130

National Library of Australia Prepublication Data Service:

A catalogue record for this book is available from the National Library of Australia

ISBN: 978 1 925467 19 2 (paperback)

Design and production by
Bill Ellemor, PenFolk Publishing

Cover design by
Bill Ellemor, PenFolk Publishing

Cover illustrations by
Lucila Zentner

written by a child survivor
of the 1983 Ash Wednesday bushfires,
for the children of
Australia's 2019–20 Black Summer

Morning Mist.

Cool damp air.

A walk uphill from wooden huts.

The lodge emerges from the cloud.

Hewn logs, a shingled roof.

A place to care for nature.

Built many years before.

Breakfast early for a day on the trails.

Camera. Notebook.

Sturdy shoes.

Choose a packed lunch.

Inscribe your name in the book.

Soft green trails underfoot.

Step gently on the forest floor.

Tullawallal, Coomera Falls.

Hear the rushing water.

Ancient ferns. Orchids. Moss.

Bellbird Lookout, tired legs.

“Can you see Egg Rock?”

Sunset resting on the terrace.

Views across a valley; beyond forever.

Before you know it, end of day.

Tummy rumbling. It's dinner-time!

"Go on kids, pull the rope."

***Clang Clang*. *Clang Clang*. Rings the Binna Burra bell.**

Friends gather, old and new.

Together, at big long tables.

A pot of soup and a buffet roast.

Share the day's adventures.

"Did you see any Little Brown Birds?"

An early start—abseiling today!

Down the rock face.

Friends wait to catch, below.

Buckles tight, lean right back.

“You can do it.”

After lunch, the Flying Fox.

Whizzing through the tree tops.

Climb back up, and go again.

A sound in the distance calls us home.

***Clang Clang*. *Clang Clang*.**

Supper in the library.

Hot chocolate and marshmallows.

Cupboards full of board games.

Walls that seem made of books.

Someone is giving a talk.

“Can anyone work the projector?”

Sleepy morning.

Warm and humid.

Try bush tucker, make some damper.

Choose your blindfold, hold the rope.

Walk the Senses Trail.

Sit still and breathe in.

Lemon Myrtle. Just like a lemonade icy-pole.

Sit still and listen.

"Can you hear the Whip Bird?"

***Eeeeeeeey-whup*.**

Saturday night, a Binna Burra bush dance.

Jeans and T-shirt, dressed just fine.

Clear a space, push back the couches.

"Watch out for the piano!"

Clap your hands and strip the willow.

One last adventure this time round.

A night-time walk in the forest.

Shine a torch and follow your guide.

Step softly.

Wait.

“Can you see the potoroo?”

Supper after.

Then hugs farewell.

“See you again next year.”

Decades fade, but memories last.

Echoes of two intrepid men.

“Time to go. The forest is dry and changing.”

Night falls and silence comes.

Wind.

Smoke.

Flames.

The lodge is returned to the mountain.

Morning mist.

Cool damp air.

Newfound friends.

And a hidden gem.

Found among the ashes.

Gently carried and held aloft.

***Clang Clang*. *Clang Clang*. Rings the Binna Burra bell.**

It's dinner time once more.

About Binna Burra Cultural Landscape and the Binna Burra Foundation

A long time ago, in the 1930s, two friends Romeo Lahey and Arthur Groom, met during the formation of the National Parks Association of Australia. A few years later, they built a guesthouse at Lamington. That guesthouse became Binna Burra Lodge. A famous spot in Queensland where people from everywhere come to enjoy nature and learn about history. The Binna Burra Cultural Landscape is listed on the Queensland Heritage Register because of its importance. The Binna Burra Cultural Landscape sits in the surrounding UNESCO-listed Gondwana rainforests.

In the wake of the 2019–20 bushfires, the Binna Burra Foundation was formed by community members to support conservation activities that protect the Binna Burra Cultural Landscape and surrounding area.

Binna Burra is part of the traditional lands of the Yugambeh Language Region of South East Queensland. The Foundation works with and acknowledges the families of the Yugambeh Language Region of South East Queensland and pays respect to Elders past, present and emerging.

Many years ago, the Shay Bell was on a train used at a sawmill in Canungra. Later, it was used as a dinner bell at Binna Burra Lodge, calling guests to meals for many, many years! The bell was recovered from the remains of the lodge after the Black Summer fires of 2019–20. The bell will take pride of place in the rebuilt lodge.

The publication of this book is proudly funded by the Gambling Community Benefit Fund. The Foundation hopes readers will gain an understanding of Binna Burra and how special it is from this book.

Afterword

The Black Summer fires impacted many Australian communities. The fires changed people's lives and reshaped many habitats, including the rainforests surrounding Binna Burra.

With these very difficult and sad times, there also came kindness and resolve. And with time and care, nature has started to renew.

The finding of the original Shay Bell reminds us that despite the difficulties of the Black Summer, Binna Burra will have a new chapter. It will again be a place where families gather and where friendships are made. A place where people are brought together by a shared concern for nature and heritage.

This book celebrates the very special place the original Binna Burra lodge was to many Queenslanders and to people who visited from around the world. It encourages readers to reflect on their own memories. It also invites readers to look to the future and continue the tradition of fellowship that has been part of Binna Burra throughout its history.

I hope many readers will create new memories with their families and friends at Binna Burra. And if you hear the bell ringing—it must be dinner time!

Her Excellency the Honourable Dr Jeannette Young AC PSM,
Governor of Queensland

Proceeds from any sales of this book will go to the Binna Burra Foundation. The author and illustrator have elected to forgo royalties to maximise the benefit to the Foundation. The Foundation would like to acknowledge the in-kind support of all involved in this project, and congratulates the illustrator on being a finalist in the 2025 Archibald Prize.